T0209569

There Is Hope
with T n T

Powerful Daily Devotional
That Never Stops Igniting

Angela Dee

WESTBOW
P R E S S®
A DIVISION OF THOMAS NELSON
& ZONDERVAN

THE HOLY BIBLE, NEW INTERNATIONAL VERSION®, NIV® Copyright © 1973, 1978, 1984, 2011 by Biblica, Inc.® Used by permission. All rights reserved worldwide.

WestBow Press books may be ordered through booksellers or by contacting:

WestBow Press
A Division of Thomas Nelson & Zondervan
1663 Liberty Drive
Bloomington, IN 47403
www.westbowpress.com
1 (866) 928-1240

ISBN: 978-1-9736-5357-8 (sc)
ISBN: 978-1-9736-5356-1 (e)

Print information available on the last page.

WestBow Press rev. date: 04/11/2019

About the Author

Christian song writer Angela Dee can relate to addiction, weakness, brokenness, anger, fear, anxiety, rejection, deception, poor choices and challenges of temptation, while being in a pit and growing up in a dysfunctional home.

Since then, Angela has found Tools of Truth (T n T) which are effective, mighty and powerful, to see her through her daily struggles and battles. Angela faces each day knowing that there will be ups and downs, yet handles them with T n T. She now relies on God and His Word, as He changes everything!

Angela Dee is passionate about sharing these tools with you that changed her dark past into a bright future.

Enjoy an instrumental C D featuring piano, flute, birds and waves for quiet time or meditation, available on Amazon called LINGER by Angie Deidesheimer.

This book is dedicated to:

To my three little buddies, Shaylee, Melia and
Gaige. You brought me unexpected joy through
unfavorable circumstances. I love you guys!

To Jackie, who gave up her life to give these children
everything she possibly could, and more. You are amazing!

To my family and friends, who sent up countless prayers
along with providing for our needs. What an incredible
Blessing you are! Each of you is a Treasured Gift!

To Jesus, for seeing us through. You are
faithful! THANK YOU LORD!

Introduction

I'm so excited that you chose this book to read! I have been praying for those who stroll through the pages. My prayer is that God does a work in you, as you journey through your past, present and future. We're not strong enough to walk alone, nor does God want that for us.

In this book, you will discover the power (T n T, which are tools of truth) to see you through life's struggles. God is not finished with you yet! He loves you! You matter to Him! He values you no matter what you have done, or what you are still digging yourself out of.

PSALM 34:5

Those who look to him are radiant; their
faces are never covered with shame.

Enjoy a list of songs at the end of each message that complements the thought of the day. Feel free to listen to them during meditation and time of worship. They are available on YouTube.

Hope Found in Jesus Being Appointed to be Head Over Everything

EPHESIANS 1:22

God placed all things under his feet and appointed him to be head over everything for the church, which is his body, the fullness of him who fills everything in every way.

JOHN 14:13

I will do whatever you ask in my name, so that the Son may bring glory to the Father.

Right here is where we begin to learn just how powerful Jesus is! The name of Jesus is the source in which we shall end all prayer time and add a touch of love and gratitude for what He has done, what he is doing and what He is about to do. He is our Power, our Savior, our Source, our All! I ask you to close your eyes a moment and meditate on what you are about to learn through God Breathed Scripture that you will be reading in this book, along with praying and spending time with the Source of life. Jesus is alive in our hearts if we have accepted Him as Lord and Savior. (We'll talk more about that later).

We all have situations in our lives where we need help; Even bosses, presidents, teachers, pastors, judges, lawyers, parents, just everyone! We need direction and clarity as well. No one is exempt or without sin, weakness, flaws, bad choices, and mistakes. I believe that you will become strong individuals as you connect with Jesus through prayer and scripture along with tools in this book.

~ PRAYER MAY BE SOMETHING LIKE THIS: Jesus, have Your way in me. Teach me to discern Your Word. Not so much this book but Your Holy Word, the Bible. Be with me as I learn from Your Word. This book is a tool of truth, which I pray will help me become the person You want me to be. I ask that You guide me on my journey with You, my Savior and Source of life. In Your Precious Name I pray Jesus, With Love and Thanksgiving.

SONGS

No Other Name by Hillsong Worship
What A Beautiful Name by Hillsong Worship
Your Great Name by Natalie Grant
There Is Power by Lincoln Brewster
In Christ Alone by Travis Cottrell

Hope Found in Spite of Our Brokeness

We are all broken! Each one of us has a weakness or situation in our lives that is unfavorable. The good news is that Jesus is not finished with us! He won't be finished with us until He calls us home to heaven. He is creating something new in us each and every day, for His glory (expression of excellence of His being). He is also the worker of miracles. He is powerful! He is the treasure inside our hearts! He is molding us daily. So don't give up! Take one day at a time. One hour at a time. In the mean-time, we have to trust Him and ask Him to show us what "we" can do to walk in His will in spite of our messy lives on this journey we call life here on earth.

2 CORINTHIANS 4:7

We have this treasure in jars of clay to show that this all-surpassing power is from God and not from us.

ISAIAH 64:8

Yet, O LORD, you are our Father. We are the clay, you are the potter; we are all the work of your hand.

~ PRAYER MAY BE SOMETHING LIKE THIS: God, mold me into what You want me to be. I can't do this on my own. I surrender my broken self to You. Show me how to get through this journey. Give me steps to take and prayers to pray. Give me the tools I need for my unique situation. Give me wisdom. Give me clarity God. Make a way. Have Your Holy way in me for Your glory. In Jesus Name I Pray, With Love and Thanksgiving.

Read the Bible to get closer to God, every day, if possible. He loves you, and wants to have a relationship with you, through His Word and His Son, Jesus Christ, who died for our sins. Talk with Him. Share every detail of your life with him. He is your best friend. He already knows what is going on and He isn't surprised! He is always there to listen. He's waiting for you. ☺

If He loves me In ALLLL my mess, He Is Crazy about You! Now Smile Big! Bigger!

SONGS

Cornerstone by (Live) by Hillsong Worship
Sweetly Broken by Jeremy Riddle
Broken by Matthew West
Held by Natalie Grant
Broken Vessels by Hillsong Worship
Gracefully Broken by Matt Redman
Dear Younger Me by MercyMe
Break Every Chain by Jesus Culture
Not Today by Hillsong United

Hope Found in Praying

Have you been taught how to pray? I know that I am guilty of just babbling on and on! Our Father knows what we need before we ask him, yet he does want us to present our requests to Him, so we acknowledge our need for him, for he is holy! This prayer below is straight from Jesus (as He teaches how to pray and what to pray for).

MATTHEW 6:9-13

Our Father in heaven, hallowed be your name, your kingdom come, your will be done on earth as it is in heaven. Give us today our daily bread. Forgive us our debts, as we also have forgiven our debtors. And lead us not into temptation, but deliver us from the evil one.

1 THESSALONIANS 5:17

Pray continually

If Jesus is going to teach me how I ought to pray, I'm on board! What about you? He wants us to proclaim Him as our father first, and that He alone is Holy! He "Himself" teaches us how we ought to pray. He knew that we needed this teaching even before He went to be with His Father in Heaven. How thoughtful of Him to think of us! He says to pray for His kingdom to come and His will to be done in our lives. Scripture tells us also, to pray continually, or without ceasing! I know ~ how can one pray day in and day out without stopping? Well, let's practice praying (or continual communication with Him) all the day through, everywhere we go, and as often as possible. This is a way to come into a relationship with Him. Apparently He wants to converse with us (yes even us sinful, earthly people), not only when we "need" Him but when we genuinely "want" Him. . Don't you get excited when you receive a text or a phone call from a loved one? Well, I believe that He gets excited when we approach Him with anything that is going on in our lives. It doesn't have to be just the big stuff and needs. He loves the little stuff as well. Just as we like the little things that our loved ones do in our own lives! You get the picture. . . How can prayers get answered without asking? He is there to answer prayers and show us His glory! We have to believe that miracles still happen as well, my friend! I need this reminder. Don't you? The Lord is faithful! He knows what today and the future hold, so we need to pray for His will, not ours! Pray to be fed, so we acknowledge whose hand feeds us. . . .Pray for forgiveness as well as forgiving those who have done us wrong. .This is sooo hard for me (maybe you too), but there is freedom when we can forgive, yet we can be held hostage by other's sins against us or who have offended us…ugg!! We don't want that! We need to continually be in communication with Him about temptation and evil, again, so He can show us His glory! We never know when the enemy is going to strike! Anytime that I have not fallen into the "temptation trap", I give Him glory, honor and praise all the day through because I know

Angela Dee

it is He who goes before me. I even count my blessings while trying to fall asleep. . Talk about a great way to fall asleep! Because I know it is Jesus who delivers me. . THANK YOU, JESUS!

This is God's kingdom and His power and His glory. He's got us, but sometimes we have to wait on Him and His will in our lives to get our prayers answered. Yes I know ~ that's not always easy, yet it's always best.

~ PRAYER MAY BE SOMETHING LIKE THIS: Father in heaven, you are on the throne, Oh Holy One. Thank you for this prayer and showing me how to pray and to pray continually. For I want Your will in my life to be done and not what I think I need. For you know best. Show me steps to take to walk in Your will, Father. . Also, thank you for feeding me and my loved ones. Thank You for taking care of us and providing all our needs. Thank You for feeding me spiritually as well. . . LORD, forgive me of my sins. I know I can be pretty crummy at times. Give me the strength to forgive others' who have done me wrong. . . In Your Name I Pray, With Love and Thanksgiving and To You Be the Glory, Amen.

The good news is that He's there for us (alive and well) and we can trust Him in our daily lives. . This is where we find peace. His Will is best and we need to surrender our lives to Him and build a relationship with the King of the universe! WOW! Come on! This is Jesus I'm talking about! Our Savior! Who else has done such a thing for us? Not our family and not our best friend! I know ~ it's hard to wrap our brain around! I get it! Give it some time. I challenge you to be open to the plans of your future. That it is about Him and not about us. Perhaps that will help you gain an understanding of who He is and His Will for you. Don't wait until you get it "all together", because it is Jesus who will do a work in you to get you "together" and to change you into what He calls you to be. We're weak and broken. He knows that! It may take some time. Be patient. This is good news my friend! You don't have to have it all together! He does all the work, through scripture, Bible study, prayer time, etc. (we do have to put time into being with Him then He does the rest). Is this not liberating? Are you on the dance floor yet? He will change your life, one scripture at a time. One day at a time. One circumstance at a time. . . .One Prayer at a time.

~ I raise my white flag to You Jesus
and surrender to Your Will ~

SONGS

Our Father by Hillsong Worship
Thy Will by Hillary Scott
Jesus I Believe by Big Daddy Weave
The Prayer by Celine Dion

Hope Found as Jesus Prays for Us

Are you hurting? Are you scared? Worried? Lonely, Suffering, Lost, Rejected, Angry, Forgotten, Left behind, Ignored, Lied to or Cheated on? Maybe the worst has happened to you or simply something that no-one would understand. Me too, my friend! The sad news for me is, I am the one who has done some of these things myself (I confess). I've had to do a lot of explaining, confessing and repenting (turning away from sin and turning to God). I have experienced these sad, down and out times in life, on both sides. Most of us have (sadly). . . One thing that I have learned through all of this is that hurting people hurt others. I grew up in a dis-functional home and I have learned that I myself am a hurtful individual and I have hurt others in my path along the way. I understand completely, if you have experienced an ugly time in life regardless if you have been the victim of circumstance or you were the bad guy. THERE IS HOPE! We can pray for a changed heart! We can ask Jesus to pray for us, to change us! Prayer changes lives! Actually, we should pray for those who have hurt us or offended us! I know ~ UGGG! But maybe someone prayed for me! Maybe their prayer got answered and that's how I came to know Jesus, my Lord and Savior! I may never know, but that can happen to you or anyone! I'm a changed person since I have surrendered my life to Christ. You can be as well! How we deal with our past, is how our final outcome stands. The good news is ~ Jesus prays for us! We can come to Him with whatever is on our minds. I love that He prays for us and don't forget, friend, He answers prayers as well. Sometimes we have to be patient to get prayers answered, but that doesn't mean that He's not praying for us and working things out behind the scenes.....Hang in there! There is hope and power going before us!

JOHN 17:20-26

My prayer is not for them alone. I pray also for those who will believe in me through their message, that all of them may be one, Father, just as you are in me and I am in you. May they also be in us so that the world may believe that you have sent me. I have given them the glory that you gave me, that they may be one as we are one: I in them and you in me. May they be brought to complete unity to let the world know that you sent me and have loved them even as you have loved me. Father, I want those you have given me to be with me where I am, and to see my glory, the glory you have given me because you loved me before the creation of the world. Righteous Father, though the world does not know you, I know you, and they know that you have sent me. I have made you known to them, and will continue to make you known in order that the love you have for me may be in them and that I myself may be in them.

When I'm down and out, experiencing one of these life issues, I ask Jesus, how to get through this? I don't deserve this! . . . I then hear His still small voice saying, I can relate. I was on that cross, rejected, hurting and suffering. He didn't deserve it either. However, God didn't leave Him or forsake Him. No, He used His suffering for His glory. Perhaps we can ask God how to use this ugly time in life, for His glory. That, my friend, can change our circumstances into something beautiful. I understand if you are not thinking that way. Ask God for a change of heart. Be patient! It takes time. Then maybe, just maybe, we can help others get through their circumstances just as Jesus does for us.

~ PRAYER MAY BE SOMETHING LIKE THIS: Jesus, THANK YOU for praying for me and those in my prayer life. THANK YOU for not giving up on me. THANK YOU for second chances and more. THANK YOU for loving me right where I am. I surrender my circumstances to you. Show me how I can use my circumstances for your glory. Help me get through this ugly time of life that I'm experiencing. How can I find joy again, Jesus? Show me your glory. In Your Precious Name I Pray, With Love and Thanksgiving.

SONGS

Christ Be All Around Me by Leeland
Through All Of This by Colton Dixon
(watch video)
Tremble by Mosaic

Hope Found in the Midst
of Our Strongholds

God sends his divine power to demolish our strongholds! A stronghold can be anything that keeps us from walking with God, such as gossip, stealing, murder, adultery, abortion, abusing our bodies, anger, lying, cheating, hatefulness - You get the picture! Our worldly ways can get the best of us. The good news is that we have scripture to go to, when we need a power bigger than us, to guide us.

2 CORINTHIANS 10:3b-6

We do not wage war as the world does. The weapons we fight with are not the weapons of the world. On the contrary, they have divine power to demolish strongholds. We demolish arguments and every pretension that sets itself up against the knowledge of God, and we take captive every thought to make it obedient to Christ. And we will be ready to punish every act of disobedience, once your obedience is complete.

Do you have a stronghold that you battle? Perhaps you may have more than one. I know I do! I confess my sins, daily (because strongholds are a form of sin). God wants us to recognize our sin and our need for Him. I read this scripture after I confess my sins, every morning. I then thank God for sending His Divine Power to Demolish My Strongholds. I recognize that my strongholds grow weaker, and weaker in time, as I praise His Holy Name, for going before me. His love does not weaken in spite of our strongholds. .NO WAY!

~ PRAYER MAY BE SOMETHING LIKE THIS: Father God, Thank You for going before me to demolish my strongholds. Who am I that you are mindful of me? They have such a grip on me that I can't battle them on my own. I trust that You go before me. Show me Your Glory, LORD! I wait in hope for You! In Jesus Name I Pray, With Love and Thanksgiving.

Wow ~ how can this be that our God goes before us in battle!

He loves us that much, even when we're at our worst. . . Well, we are His children you know.

Why wouldn't He help us, we're family!

SONGS

> Do It Again by Elevation Worship
> Our God by Chris Tomlin
> Our God Is The Lion by Big Daddy Weave
> I Am Not Alone by Kari Jobe

Hope Found in Waiting on The Lord

Believe it or not, we can live a joyful life, knowing that we have the Lord by our side!

Even in our dark circumstances, there is hope, my friend. I'm not saying that it is easy, but when we trust that He is with us, we can take a deep breath and say "OK God, You are my hope and shield and I can trust in You."

PSALM 33:20-22

We wait in hope for the LORD; he is our help and our shield. In him our hearts rejoice, for we trust in his holy name; May your unfailing love rest upon us, O LORD, even as we put our hope in you.

Hope, I just need some hope! What about you? It is easy to turn to people in our lives for hope, but only when we turn to our Lord, will we find hope that we can trust, because He is holy. I love that word, holy. It stands alone! Did I mention ~ He's there! People don't always have the answers that we need. He does and that is why it is necessary to stay connected to Him.

~ PRAYER MAY BE SOMETHING LIKE THIS: Okay God, I trust You, and completely, because You alone are holy. Be with me and my loved ones today and always, Lord. Go before us. Be our help and shield like no other. In Jesus Name I Pray, with Love and Thanksgiving.

SONGS

Waiting Here For You by Christy Nockels
Everlasting God by Chris Tomlin
Wait On The Lord by Donnie McClurkin

Hope Found in the Strength of the Lord

EPHESIANS 6:10-18

Finally, be strong in the Lord and in his mighty power. Put on the full armor of God so that you can take your stand against the devil's schemes. For our struggle is not against flesh and blood, but against the rulers, against the authorities, against the powers of this dark world and against the spiritual forces of evil in the heavenly realms. Therefore put on the full armor of God, so that when the day of evil comes, you may be able to stand your ground, and after you have done everything, to stand. Stand firm then, with the belt of truth buckled around your waist, with the breastplate of righteousness in place, and with your feet fitted with the readiness that comes from the gospel of peace. In addition to all this, take up the shield of faith, with which you can extinguish all the flaming arrows of the evil one. Take the helmet of salvation and the sword of the Spirit, which is the word of God. And pray in the Spirit on all occasions with all kinds of prayers and requests.

There are days when I feel that I need an army to go to battle for me. I just can't do this alone. What about you? I realize I have to pick and choose my battles, but do you ever get worn out from constantly going through the battles of life?

I get it! I truly do! The good news is that we don't have to do this in our own strength!

This scripture implies that our human strength is inadequate for battle but God's Power is invincible! Hallelujah! The battle is spiritual and must be fought in God's strength, depending on the Word and God, through prayer. He loves us more than we can imagine. He wants to hold our hand through the battles of life and give us scripture to learn how to pray, so He can see us through.

~ PRAYER MAY BE SOMETHING LIKE THIS: Oh Mighty One, King of Kings, My Warrior, Thank You for showing me that You are fighting my battles. Help me to stay focused in prayer and give me unrushed time with You. Thank you for clarifying that these battles are spiritual forces of evil. Have Your way in me as I connect with You through Your Spirit. I love You and trust You. In Jesus Name I Pray, With Love and Thanksgiving.

SONGS

Strong God by Vertical Worship
Stronger by Hillsong Worship
You Are My Strength by Hillsong Worship

Hope Found in the Possibilities of God

Did you ever find yourself in a situation that you just didn't seem to think there could be a way out of or an end to it? I sure have (I'm in one right now!) UGG!

LUKE 18:27

Jesus replied, "What is impossible with
men is possible with God."

This one is not easy to embrace. However, I have seen God work in my life, in ways that I couldn't have gotten through by myself. We have to think bigger than ourselves. First of all, God has no boundaries. There are no limits on what He can do! Our part is to pray, much. Follow God, even when we don't really feel like it, as in going to church, reading the bible, embracing bible study and even asking fellow believers to pray for us. He is on the throne and He can do it, yet I think He wants us near and dear to Him to embrace His glory. He loves us as we fully put our trust in Him and embrace His unlimited possibilities.

~ PRAYER MAY BE SOMETHING LIKE THIS: God, oh my heavenly Father, go before me and do the impossible that I am not equipped to do. You are holy! You can do it!

I need You to go before me. Jesus, will You pray for me? I need a miracle and I give You the glory for prayers answered and situations, changed. Thank You for always being there for me, even when I don't see You. I will do my best to stay connected with You during this season and all the days of my life. Jesus, will You intercede for me? In Your Name I Pray, With Love and Thanksgiving.

SONGS

I Stand In Awe by Hillsong Worship
Healer by Kari Jobe
Greater Than All by Hillsong Worship
I Just Need U by Toby Mac

Hope Found in the Holy Spirit

ACTS 2:38, 39

Peter replied, "Repent and be baptized, every one of you, in the name of Jesus Christ for the forgiveness of your sins. And you will receive the gift of the Holy Spirit. The promise is for you and your children and for all who are far off—for all whom the Lord our God will call.

ROMANS 8:5-11

Those who live according to the sinful nature have their minds set on what that nature desires; but those who live in accordance with the Spirit have their minds set on what the Spirit desires. The mind of sinful man is death, but the mind controlled by the Spirit is life and peace; the sinful mind is hostile to God. It does not submit to God's law, nor can it do so. Those controlled by the sinful nature cannot please God. You however, are controlled not by the sinful nature but by the Spirit, if the Spirit of God lives in you. And if anyone does not have the Spirit of Christ, he does not belong to Christ. But if Christ is in you, your body is dead because of sin, yet your spirit is alive because of righteousness. And if the Spirit of him who raised Jesus from the dead is living in you, he who raised Christ from the dead will also give life to your mortal bodies through his Spirit, who lives in you.

Angela Dee

ROMANS 8:26-27

In the same way, the Spirit helps us in our weakness. We do not know what we ought to pray for, but the Spirit himself intercedes for us with groans that words cannot express. And he who searches our hearts knows the mind of the Spirit, because the Spirit intercedes for the saints in accordance with God's will.

Jesus baptized us with the Spirit, by which He would cause those who believe in Him to participate in the powers and graces of the new life. (John 1:33, note NIV). If we believe in Christ, then the Spirit lives in us. This does not mean that we don't sin. I love the message in this scripture about how the mind set of believers is controlled by the Spirit, which is life and peace. I also love the scripture that says the Spirit helps us in our weakness as well as intercedes for us with groans. This is hope! We can always be hopeful knowing that we have the Spirit praying for us. This is reason to be joyful, upbeat, smiling and positive in the midst of our daily lives.

~ PRAYER MAY BE SOMETHING LIKE THIS: Holy Spirit, Thank You for interceding for me with groans and interceding for me in my weakness. You care! You care! I struggle to keep my mind off of things in this world. I ask You, Holy Spirit, to continue to pray for me and intercede for me. I plan on studying Your Word and learning more about You, Holy Spirit. Will You direct my prayer life and give me wisdom as I search for you? In Jesus Name I Pray, With Love and Thanksgiving

SONGS

Spirit Of The Living God by Vertical Worship

Open Heaven (River Wild) by Hillsong Worship

Here With Me by MercyMe

Here With You by Hillsong Worship

Holy Spirit by Francesca Battistelli

Angela Dee

Hope Found in the Midst of Anxiety

PHILIPPIANS 4:6

Do not be anxious about anything, but in everything, by prayer and petition, with thanksgiving, present your requests to God. And the peace of God, which transcends all understanding, will guard your hearts and your minds in Christ Jesus.

Anxiety, worry, fear, and sleepless nights are not a godly way to live. We need to trust God in all circumstances by praying and telling God our concerns. Anxiety is the opposite of peace, which is the tranquility that comes when believers commit all their cares to God in prayer and worry about them no more. I know for a fact that this is not easy and can take some time in prayer and petition, with thanksgiving, to lay our cares at the feet of Jesus and leave them. It's what we have to do since we don't have control over our lives. The good news is, He has control over us! We have to believe in Him and surrender our circumstances to Him and trust His Holy will in them.

You can do it - put your trust in Him. He's got it!

~ PRAYER MAY BE SOMETHING LIKE THIS: Father, I need You to take care of my concerns. I ask You to do a work in me to transform my worries into trust. I can't do this myself. Jesus, will You pray for me and intercede for me? Holy Spirit, will You intercede for me and enable me to put my trust in You? In Jesus Name I Pray, With Love and Thanksgiving.

SONGS

No Longer Slaves by Bethel Music
Fear Is A Liar by Zach Williams
You Never Let Go by Passion
I Am Not Alone by Kari Jobe

There is Hope Found in Being an Overcomer

1 JOHN 5:1-5

Everyone who believes that Jesus is the Christ is born of God, and everyone who loves the father loves his child as well. This is how we know that we love the children of God: by loving God and carrying out his commands. This is love for God: to obey his commands. And his commands are not burdensome, for everyone born of God overcomes the world. This is the victory that has overcome the world, even our faith. Who is it that overcomes the world; only he who believes that Jesus is the Son of God.

Studying God's Word helps to understand how to apply scripture to our prayer life or our lives in general. I pray that you have a Bible. A study Bible is awesome because you will find clarity, partnering with scripture that will change your life, help you understand the word and also help to live an abundant life.

I found clarity in this scripture while reading the "notes" on this scripture. They read, "This is love for God, to obey His commands. His commands are not burdensome. Not because the commands themselves are light or easy to obey but because of the new birth. The one born of God by faith is enabled by the Holy Spirit to obey.

OVERCOME ~ to overcome the world is to gain victory over its sinful pattern of life, which is another way of describing obedience to God. Such obedience is not impossible for believers because they have been born again and the Holy Spirit dwells within them and gives them strength. (notes from NIV New International Version 1 JOHN 5:3-4). This is incredible hope!

Share this hope with someone today!

~ PRAYER MAY BE SOMETHING LIKE THIS: Heavenly Father, I thank You for revealing to me through Your Word that I am an overcomer! I am reminded of the power of Your Word and the need I have for it daily. Thank You for giving me strength through Your Holy Spirit. I want what You want. Your Will in my life be done. Holy Spirit, will You intercede for me and enable me to be obedient? In Jesus Name I Pray, With Love And Thanksgiving.

SONGS

God Is Able by Hillsong Worship
Overcomer by Mandisa
Overcome (Live) by New Life Worship

Hope Found in the Many Ways
That God Shows up in Our Lives

I read this scripture every morning during my quiet time. It is loaded with so many reminders of who God is and some benefits that He has in store for those of us, who love Him.

PSALM 91

He who dwells in the shelter of the Most High will rest in the shadow of the Almighty. I will say of the LORD, "He is my refuge and my fortress, my God, in whom I trust." Surely he will save you from the fowler's snare and from the deadly pestilence. He will cover you with his feathers, and under his wings you will find refuge; his faithfulness will be your shield and rampart. You will not fear the terror of night, nor the arrow that flies by day, nor the pestilence that stalks in the darkness, nor the plague that destroys at midday. A thousand may fall at your side, ten thousand at your right hand, but it will not come near you. You will only observe with your eyes and see the punishment of the wicked. If you make the Most High your dwelling—even the LORD, who is my refuge – then no harm will befall you, no disaster will come near your tent. For he will command his angels concerning you to guard you in all your ways; they will lift you up in their hands, so that you will not strike your foot against a stone. You will tread upon the lion and the cobra;

you will trample the great lion and the serpent. "Because he loves me," says the LORD, "I will rescue him; I will protect him, for he acknowledges my name. He will call upon me, and I will answer him; I will be with him in trouble; I will deliver him and honor him. With long life will I satisfy him and show him my salvation."

Wow! He is our refuge! He saves us! He satisfies us! He delivers us and honors us! He is with us in times of trouble! He answers us! He protects us and rescues us! He even sends His angels concerning us! He is faithful and we can trust Him. I encourage you to spend some time in this scripture. Maybe you can start your day with this passage, during your quiet time. It's a great daily reminder of what God does in our lives and just how big He is. We can find tremendous encouragement here. His Word is alive and well! All we have to do is love Him and acknowledge His name. That's all we have to do! Isn't He amazing? He doesn't expect much out of us! Just to love Him and acknowledge Him! Our knee should be bending all the day long, to acknowledge His goodness, His blessings and His faithfulness!

~ PRAYER MAY BE SOMETHING LIKE THIS: Oh Most High, You are the Almighty. Thank You for this scripture that I can read daily, as a reminder of just How Big You Are and what You do for those of us who love You and acknowledge You, LORD. . I am not worthy of your goodness, God. Thank You, for every detail that You are! I love You!! Be blessed by my acknowledgement and adoration for You God. In Jesus Name I Pray, With Love and Thanksgiving.

SONGS

My Everything by Jesus Culture
Never Once by Matt Redman
Let Faith Arise by Christ Tomlin
You Are My All In All by Nichole Nordeman
God You're So Good by Passion

Hope Found in Angels

PSALM 34:7

The angel of the LORD encamps
around those who fear him.

PSALM 91:11

For he will command his angels concerning
you to guard you in all your ways;

LUKE 12:8

I tell you, whoever acknowledges me before
men; the Son of Man will also acknowledge
him before the angels of God.

What a blessing to know that angels are encamping around us! What a picture! Close your eyes and meditate on angels encamping around you. He commands His angels concerning us! A command! They are "called" to guard us in all our ways! The Son of Man, "Jesus" himself, acknowledges us before the angels of God! We have to acknowledge Jesus before men, first. What hope is here! Angels, always! I envision them all around you and me! What peace that brings to a heart!

~ PRAYER MAY BE SOMETHING LIKE THIS: Father God, Thank You for sending Your angels to encamp around me! Will You send them to encamp around my loved ones? Jesus, I will pray about making a point to acknowledge You before men. I will make an effort to let those around me know who You are. I give You glory for loving me enough to acknowledge me. Praise Your Holy Name! Jesus, will You be with me as I acknowledge You before others? In Your Name I Pray, With Love and Thanksgiving.

SONGS

Whom Shall I Fear by Chris Tomlin
Angel By Your Side by Francesca
Angel Tonight by Leigh Nash
Dancing With The Angels by Monk & Neagle

Hope Found in Confessing Our Sins

I have found that when I repent of my sins and turn to God, He creates in me, a different human being. I'm not saying that I don't sin anymore, but He does a work in me, to not want to sin. . In other words, I hang with folks who follow Him (as I try), and we do life together. We pray for one another as we do our best to walk in His Will and stay away from traps of this fallen world. We encourage one another, go to church together, or meet at Bible study or other small group. We're there to help each other out.

PSALM 51:1-12

Have mercy on me, O God, according to your unfailing love; according to your great compassion; blot out my transgressions. Wash away all my iniquity and cleanse me from my sin; for I know my transgressions, and my sin is always before me. Against you, you only, have I sinned and done what is evil in your sight, so that you are proved right when you speak and justified when you judge. Surely I was sinful at birth, sinful from the time my mother conceived me. Surely you desire truth in the inner parts; you teach me wisdom in the inmost place. Cleanse me with hyssop, and I will be clean; wash me, and I will be whiter than snow. Let me hear joy and gladness; let the bones you have crushed rejoice. Hide your face from my sins and blot out all my iniquity. Create in me a pure heart, O God, and renew a steadfast spirit within me. Do not cast me from your presence or take your Holy Spirit from me. Restore to me the joy of your salvation and grant me a willing spirit to sustain me.

I confess my sins daily, first thing in the morning and oh, and what a list I have, my friend! I have found that when He disciplines me, I come out a better and stronger person than before. I'm not proud of sin, yet I am reminded of how much He still loves me, wants to have a relationship with me, and my need for Him. He wouldn't discipline me if he didn't love me. That's one way he shows how he cares for me. Can you relate? That is what the cross is about. He forgave me and you. He forgives us, still! This is where I find my joy to follow Him. He doesn't need me, but I sure need Him. He loves you and me no matter what. I don't care where we were or where we still are. This is why I am crazy about Him and love Him with an undying love and want to serve Him and walk in His will. He loves us deeply and unconditionally.

~ PRAYER MAY BE SOMETHING LIKE THIS: Oh Jesus, I'm a mess! I have not honored your Word. I have not honored You with my heart. I have not honored You in my relationships, in my marriage, in parenting. I have not honored the Sabbath. I have not honored You with my body, with my life and my lifestyle etc. Will You forgive me? Thank You God, for sending Your Son into the world to love us and not condemn us. Thank You Jesus, for going to the cross for my sins. Thank You Jesus for your mercy and thank You for your grace. Thank You that your mercies are new every day. Thank You for making me right with God. I don't deserve You, yet I want to follow You and serve You, You only. I Love You! God, Thank You For Your Unlimited Patience. Will You do a work in me to change, for Your will to be done in me? In Your Name I Pray, Jesus, With Love and Thanksgiving.

SONGS

Lead Me To The Cross by Hillsong Worship
Come To The Altar by Elevation Worship
Life Defined by Shane & Shane

Hope Found in His Grace

Here is a scripture that I struggle to accept for
myself. Let's see if you struggle with it!

2 CORINTHIANS 12:9

"My grace is sufficient for you, for my
power is made perfect in weakness."

Grace ~ we all need it, yet do we embrace it? We certainly
don't deserve it! I struggle receiving it, because I don't feel
good enough, strong enough or even (un-sinful) enough.
Scripture tells us that the apostle Paul had a thorn. I feel
as though I have many thorns! How about you? Do you
struggle with trying to get it right all of the time or even
some of the time? No matter how hard I try, I just seem to
fall short. When I really mess up, (and I mean "big time"
mess up), I find myself on my knees again, praying about
something that I have messed up, over and over again! Can
you relate?

God gives us grace when we don't deserve it, and we need
to accept it! Grace is "unmerited favor." Human weakness
provides the ideal opportunity for the display of divine
power. I'm not suggesting that sin is okay, and I'm not
suggesting taking advantage of His grace. However, I am

quoting scripture where He, The Big Guy says, "My grace is sufficient for you, for my power is made perfect in weakness". Let's receive it, keep it, and extend it, when others fall short. They deserve it too! He loves us no matter what! We cannot be so weak for Him to turn His back on us. We are beautiful in His eyes and He's not even surprised when we mess up and mess up big time, friend! I have found that when I praise God, while caught up in the midst of needing His grace, He somehow pursues me, shows up and even follows me and yes, goes before me. I know this sounds crazy, but when I have nothing to offer, with my broken contrite heart and empty hands, He reminds me that I am His, and His love NEVER ends. Now my soul sings, " Your Love, it Knows No End", and I'm back in His arms with unspeakable joy! How about you? Is your soul singing? I sure hope so! Receive His grace today. It's a gift. Receive it, unwrap it and treasure it. Give it away when someone else needs a gift. What a beautiful thing! It can change a life.

~ PRAYER MAY BE SOMETHING LIKE THIS: Jesus, thank You for Your unmerited favor. How can You love me like You do? Thank You for Your grace. Thank You for understanding my weakness. How can I ever repay You for what You do for me? Maybe I can start by receiving Your grace, since it is a gift. Help me to extend grace to others as needed. It's in Your Holy Precious Name I Pray, With Love and Thanksgiving.

SONGS

This Is Our God by Hillsong Worship
Amazing Grace (My Chains Are Gone) by
Chris Tomlin
Majesty (Here I am) by Delirious
Your Grace Finds Me by Matt Redman
This Is Amazing Grace by Phil Wickham

Hope Found in Justice

ROMANS 8:1-2

Therefore, there is now no condemnation for those who are in Christ Jesus, because through Christ Jesus the law of the Spirit of life set me free from the law of sin and death.

This is amazing hope! We all can have a brighter day, a brighter future knowing and believing that we are not condemned through the blood of Jesus Christ, who set us free from the law of sin and death. Our sin is forgotten! We're forgiven! Our soul is without blemish! We are chosen, not forsaken. We are His and we are freed from all sin! Our debt is paid!!

Can I get an Amen! Hallelujah! Shouts of praise and then some!

~ PRAYER MAY BE SOMETHING LIKE THIS: Thank you Jesus! Thank you Jesus! Thank you Jesus!

SONGS

Child Of God by Hillsong Worship
Loyal by Lauren Daigle
You're Beautiful by MercyMe

Hope Found in Forgiveness

MATTHEW 6:14

For if you forgive men when they sin against you,
your heavenly Father will also forgive you.

I must admit, this is such a hard thing to do! Do you struggle to forgive those who offend you? I have found myself praying and praying to God to help me to forgive those who have offended me. We can be kept in bondage when we don't forgive others. Jesus doesn't want that for us. He wants us to live a joyful life, not an angry, sad life. I know of someone who was sexually abused by her own father more than 200 times, yet she found her peace when she forgave him. That's freedom! I always look to the cross and meditate on what Jesus did for me, when I have a hard time with forgiveness. This helps as I remember that He forgives me when I don't deserve it. That inspires me to forgive, when they don't deserve it. I did not say anything about this being easy. It's not! However, we are called to forgive. Have you done anything that you should be forgiven for? I thought so, me too. Thank You, Jesus, for forgiving us and loving us even when we can be sinful and stubborn in our own pride.

~ PRAYER MAY BE SOMETHING LIKE THIS: Jesus, Thank You once again for the cross and for forgiving me my wrongs. I am having a hard time forgiving those who have done me wrong. If I'm honest, I have a hard time forgiving myself, Lord. Yes, even myself. Will You do a work in me and help me to forgive as You forgive? Thank You Jesus! It's in Your Precious Name I Pray, With Love and Thanksgiving.

SONGS

Forgiveness by Mathew West
Losing by Tenth Avenue North
Love Ran Red by Chris Tomlin

Hope Found in Knowing
What Love Is

1 JOHN 3:16-18

This is how we know what love is: Jesus Christ laid down
his life for us. And we ought to lay down our lives for
our brothers. If anyone has material possessions and sees
his brother in need but has no pity on him, how can the
love of God be in him? Dear children, let us not love
with words or tongue but with actions and in truth.

HOSEA 14:4

I will heal their waywardness and love them freely, for my
anger has turned away from them.

He's not mad at us. He's not a bit angry. However, we have
to let him in, to heal us. We must accept Him and not run
from Him. This is love, my friend.

Do you find it hard to love everyone around you? If so,
then you are normal. We must pray for Jesus to do a work
in us to love everyone and deeply. I have found that when I
am honest with God and ask Him to do a work in me, He
does it over time. We can get caught up in peoples' little
quirks. They can get on our nerves and make us turn the

other way! Just be aware that you and I can get on peoples' nerves as well. Really? YES! The good news is, Jesus can do a work in us and as time goes by, we find that, Yes, we "can" love deeply and accept folks and their quirks. This is how we know that we belong to the Truth and how we set our hearts on our Savior, our Master, and King and hopefully, over time, others will want to be like us. Not because "we" love deeply but they will see Jesus in us. If that's not enough to get you motivated, then ponder the cross, where Jesus laid down His life for you and me. We owe Him our lives, our love, our all! Close your eyes and meditate on how much He must love you, no matter what, friend. Soak in His unconditional love. Bathe in Him giving up His own life, laying down His life for you. You are worth it! Receive it! How can you give away love, if you haven't first received it? It's a gift. Maybe that's where you can start. Start by receiving His love today and then pray about passing it on unconditionally, deeply, whole heartedly. LOVE WINS EVERY TIME!

~ PRAYER MAY BE SOMETHING LIKE THIS: Jesus, Thank You for loving me and accepting me just the way I am. I am not worthy, but You are worthy. Do a work in me to love others unconditionally, Jesus. I admit that I struggle in this area. I want people to see You in me. Thank You for laying Your life down for me, Jesus. I owe You my life. I owe You my love. I owe it to You, Jesus, to love the world that You love. I ask You to do a work in me, Jesus. In Your Holy Name I Pray, With Love and Thanksgiving.

SONGS

Love Knows No End by Hillsong Worship
Reckless Love by Cory Asbury
Fierce by Jesus Culture
Be Love by Plus One
Jesus He Loves Me by Chris Tomlin
How Deep The Father's Love by Nicole
Nordeman

Hope Found When We
Don't Judge Others

MATTHEW 7:1

"Do not judge, or you too will be judged. For in the same way you judge others, you will be judged, and with the measure you use, it will be measured to you."

OUCH! Guilty here! God has done a HUGE work in me to make a stand not to judge others. It seems that I can judge others simply because they may be different from me, or think different, or dress different, or be highly educated, (which can make me feel inferior). I may even think, their sin is evident or less evident (they have it all together), and it makes me feel uncomfortable around them! What about you? Have you been in my shoes, judging or even gossiping about others, or maybe something else? Aren't we all guilty? What I like about this scripture is that it teaches us to accept others for who they are, regardless of their color, ethnicity, or background. We don't necessarily have to agree with them, but for me, I have found that life is much easier to live in a nonjudgmental frame of mind, while embracing the differences we all have. Actually, maybe weird can be a beautiful thing! We don't know where people have come from, yet we can think they're weird at times. Perhaps we're all weird to someone! To be honest with you ~ we all battle insecurities of some sort now and then, wishing we were different. I know I sure do! This can be a real issue at times! Do you ever think like that? Do you wish you were different or could change something about yourself? I have learned to be content and even embrace my "stuff". I pray that you can as well, friend. I love that God made us all different! What a colorful world I have come to love, embrace and even appreciate! How boring life would be if we all were the same. Close your eyes a minute and meditate on God forming you, creating His best, with many possibilities, just the way He planned, with no blemishes in His eyes. I challenge us all to make an effort to see others as God sees them. What a different world this could be!

~ PRAYER MAY BE SOMETHING LIKE THIS: Oh my God, I have judged when I didn't even realize that I judged! Thank You for this scripture, God. Thank you for pointing this out to me. Will you do a work in me to help me see people through Your eyes and embrace what You create? I am sorry for not giving You credit for how others are made. I ask that You enable me to love and even embrace this colorful world that You create, even myself, Lord. I seem to pick myself apart at times, and now I pray that I can accept myself just how You made me. You don't make junk, Lord. Thank You for me! Thank You for them! Will You see me through this process of a changed heart? In Jesus Name I Pray, With Love and Thanksgiving.

SONGS

You Say by Lauren Daigle
You Are More by Tenth Avenue North
Remind Who I Am by Jason Gray

Hope Found When We Love God

DEUTERONOMY 6:5-9

Love the LORD your God with all your heart and with all your soul and with all your strength. These commandments that I give you today are to be upon your hearts. Impress them on your children. Talk about them when you sit at home and when you walk along the road, when you lie down and when you get up. Tie them as symbols on your hands and bind them on your foreheads. Write them on the doorframes of your houses and on your gates.

What an awesome scripture! You can just hear God's voice speaking right to your heart. He knows how difficult life is for us. Maybe that's why he gave us such important wisdom to share with our children. He says to talk about His love and commandments, 24/7, because He knows that we can slip away in just a blink of an eye. I slipped away for a long while, I lived an immoral life style. I didn't know Him. I did not know that He loved me. I didn't know His Word (the Bible and His truth). Now I know Him personally and love Him with all my heart and more! My children know Him personally as well. We aim to please Him and honor Him as well as include Him in all areas of our lives, as we are surviving in His grace. He is worth loving deeply! His commandments are solid to stand on. Our conversations about Him are exciting and vibrant because we share what He does in our daily lives. This love is not boring. This love is real, alive and thriving and you can have it too, my friend. He wants to do life with you, have a relationship with you, love you and receive your love back. He created us for His enjoyment, not to just watch us live an aimless life without Him. We owe it to Him to love Him, to include Him in our daily lives and embrace his affection for us, just as we enjoy our loved ones. This is a 2-way love commitment, just as our love relationships are here on earth. You are the apple of His eye, you know. He is crazy about you! You matter to Him! After all ~ Jesus hung on that cross, with wide open arms, to show us just how much He loves you and me. It's a beautiful thing!

~ PRAYER MAY BE SOMETHING LIKE THIS: Father God, Daddy, I love you! I'm going to teach my children about You. I'm going to teach them to love You with all their heart. I'm ready to include You in all areas of my life. Guide me through this relationship with You. I want to know You, personally and do life with You from this moment on. Be with me always. In Jesus Name I Pray, With Love and Thanksgiving.

SONGS

Depths by Hillsong Worship
Inside Out by Hillsong Worship
Love You More by Nichole Nordeman
Thank You Jesus by Hillsong Worship

Hope Found in Swallowing
Our Pride

There are times when we take pride being in leadership, whether it is in a large corporation or a small company, a group, a home, a church, a club we may be proud of, how we think, what we put into our bodies or even build them! The list is endless! It can be an "all about me" world or self-centered dominion.

PROVERBS 11:2

When pride comes, then disgrace comes,
but with humility comes wisdom.

PROVERBS 16:18

Pride goes before destruction, a haughty spirit before a fall.

PROVERBS 8:13

To fear the LORD is to hate evil: I hate pride and arrogance, evil behavior and perverse speech.

I love these scriptures! Here is a clear image of how God is for us and not against us. He wants the best for us! He gives us the scripture to live by, so we live the abundant life that He plans for us! He knows how easy it is to follow the peer pressure of this world. To be honest, we don't even realize that pride is the reason that we are living a damaged lifestyle. Pride goes before us to wreck our relationships, our marriages, our jobs, our bodies, our churches, our future, and the list goes on and on. The good news is that He tells us to humble ourselves and get into His Word (Wisdom), to give us direction on how to live a fruitful, joyful, abundant life. We won't know TRUTH unless we get into The Word. He's got your back and He's got mine.

Tip ~ if you want to know if you have pride in your life; just take a moment and meditate on your sin, that my friend, will humble you (and me).

~ PRAYER MAY BE SOMETHING LIKE THIS: Father God, I thank You for pointing out my pride. I didn't even realize that I am living a prideful life and I can't change without owning it. Will you forgive me for my self-centered attitude? Speak to me through scripture and show me how to live this abundant life that You have planned for me. In Jesus Name I Pray, With Love and Thanksgiving.

SONGS

Heart Of Worship by Matt Redman
Jesus Lover Of My Soul by Kari Jobe
Not To Us by Nicole Nordeman
Lay Me Down by Chris Tomlin

HOPE FOUND IN SUBMITTING OURSELVES TO GOD

JAMES 4:7–8a

Submit yourselves, then, to God. Resist the
devil, and he will flee from you. Come near
to God and he will come near to you.

You may be thinking to yourself, "Ha, I have been trying
to resist the devil for quite some time"! Well, when was the
last time that you told God that you submit to Him? If you
have, then continue to tell him daily. Also, ask Jesus to pray
for you, intercede for you, to resist the enemy and to come
near God. Ask the Holy Spirit to intercede for you as well as
enable you to resist the devil. The more praying for us, the
more prayers go up. Read this scripture daily. You may even
want to memorize it and proclaim it all the day through.
He gives these scriptures to us because He wants the best
for us and knows how weak we are. That is love, my friend!

~ PRAYER MAY BE SOMETHING LIKE THIS: I submit
myself to You God. Jesus, will You pray for me and intercede
for me to resist the devil? Holy Spirit, will You intercede for
me and enable me to resist the enemy? Thank You for all
that You have done and all that You are about to do. In Your
Precious Name I Pray, Jesus, With Love and Thanksgiving.

SONGS

Come As You Are by Crowder
Love On The Line by Hillsong Worship
My Heart Is Yours by Passion
Surrender by Hillsong Worship
Brave by Nichole Nordeman

Hope Found in Praise and Worship

PSALM 150:2, 6

Praise him for his acts of power; praise
him for his surpassing greatness.

If you woke up today; there is reason to PRAISE THE
LORD. If you opened your eyes today; there is reason
to PRAISE THE LORD! We can take for granted the
provisions that we have, 24/7 (because they are just part of
everyday life). Oh, they can be taken away in a flash! They are
NOT just a part of everyday life! They are a gift! Just think
a minute. He gives us the air we breathe, the sun to warm
us, as well as garnishing the sky with miraculous sunrises
and sunsets to relish. He provides rain that we sometimes
whine about and the moon to enjoy as our own personal
night light. He nourishes the gardens to feed us, along with
a grocery store nearby that has the food practically prepared
for us! This is good stuff! I have a friend with a disease who
cannot swallow. Have you ever thought what life would be
like if you couldn't even swallow or cough, etc.? You get
the picture. I could go on and on but I'll spare you. We can
sometimes get caught up in the negative things in our lives.
They consume us! We all have them, yet if we can change
our hearts and fix our thoughts on what we "have", instead
of what we DON'T have, we can live joyfully and appreciate

this abundant life He has gifted us with. We need to pray about seeing the glass half full instead of half empty! We need to PRAISE THE LORD all day long, even when we wake in the middle of the night, for the little things in life, as well as the big things.

Close your eyes a minute and meditate on the things He does for you and your loved ones. Things you have on a daily basis. Things you receive once a week or once a month or even once a year. These are gifts from the Giver Himself! You and yours are most precious to Him! Chew on that a minute. He loves you! He cares for you! Let's make the most out of what we have and celebrate His abundance! Honestly, it should be an honor to praise His Holy Name, no matter what season of life we're in. Let's receive our gifts with a cheerful heart. We don't deserve them, yet He blesses us anyway. This should cause permanent joy and raised hands in worship.

May I say that I am sorry if you are not feeling blessed and are down and out. I am sooo sorry, friend. I have been there as well. The truth is, we shouldn't stay there. You can't move forward, by staying put. As hard as it can be, tune in to Christian radio or television. Sometimes there are folks who call in, with stories that you can relate to. They are also loaded with encouraging messages or songs. Maybe in due time, you will find joy again, to PRAISE THE LORD.

Here's a tip - You can't PRAISE THE LORD for the good stuff while your mind is on the bad stuff (because your mind is on the good stuff, blessings, prayers answered, etc.)

So keep on Praising and soon the things of this world will grow strangely dim.

~ PRAYER MAY BE SOMETHING LIKE THIS: Oh Father, I didn't realize the gifts You place in my life. They are precious! I didn't think of them as gifts from You. You are good to me and those around me. I am truly blessed! I am now going to meditate on how much You really DO love me and care for me and my loved ones. From this day forward, I shall live in abundance of Your grace and thank You all day for everything You give me, do for me and bless me with. I shall praise You all of my days, God. I will give glory to You for all You are, In Jesus Name.

SONGS

Here I Am To Worship by Matt Redman
Jesus Son Of God by Chris Tomlin
Great Are You Lord by All Sons & Daughters
Ever Be (Live) by Kalley Heiligenthal/ Bethel Music
Great I Am by Phillips, Craig & Dean
Overwhelmed by Big Daddy Weave
Revelation Song by Kari Jobe
God You Reign by Lincoln Brewster
How Great Is Our God by Chris Tomlin
How Great Thou Art by Carrie Underwood

Hope Found Going to Church

PSALM 92

It is good to praise the LORD and make music to your name, O Most High, to proclaim your love in the morning and your faithfulness at night, to the music of the ten-stringed lyre and the melody of the harp. For you make me glad by your deeds, O LORD; I sing for joy at the works of your hands. How great are your thoughts! The senseless man does not know, fools do not understand, that though the wicked spring up like grass and all evildoers flourish; they will be forever destroyed. But you, O LORD are exalted forever. For surely your enemies, O LORD, surely your enemies will perish; all evildoers will be scattered. You have exalted my horn like that of a wild ox, fine oils have been poured upon me. My eyes have seen the defeat of my adversaries; my ears have heard the rout of my wicked foes. The righteous will flourish like a palm tree, they will grow like a cedar of Lebanon; planted in the house of the LORD, they will still bear fruit in old age, they will stay fresh and green, proclaiming, "The LORD is upright; he is my Rock and there is no wickedness in him."

HEBREWS 10:25

*Let us not give up meeting together, as some are in
the habit of doing, but let us encourage one another—
and all the more as you see the Day approaching.*

Here we have another scripture that calls us to praise
the Lord and for a good reason! He alone stands for His
faithfulness, His deeds, His works and His thoughts. He is
sure to destroy all evildoers and enemies. That my friend is
reason to raise our voices to the heavens and beyond! We,
the righteous, are promised to flourish and even in old age.
That is exciting to me, because I am older and still need
purpose in my life, until He calls me home. What about
you? Can you relate to this scripture? Do you get excited
enough to go to church, get connected with other believers
and praise the Lord? I sure hope so. The church is a good
place to be! Now, don't worry if you don't feel good enough
to even step into a church, my friend, because the church is
a hospital for the sick and not a four wall building for those
who have it all together, because frankly, no one does. In
other words; you and I don't have to have it "all together"
to go to church. Also, isn't He worth it? He is worthy! Bring
a friend or go by yourself, like I do. I can assure you that it
will be worth it! I always leave church being thankful that
I went because of the message I received and the songs of
worship that always refresh my total being, while being in
the presence of our Holy One! I challenge you to seek a
church. Don't give up if you don't find the church you are
looking for. Go seek out a few churches, or more, to find the

right fit for you. New relationships await you along with a chance to serve and be refreshed!

~ PRAYER MAY BE SOMETHING LIKE THIS: I have strayed for too long, Lord. Will you guide me to the place where You would have me go to church? I know they are all different, so help me seek out the church that is a good fit for me. I may not praise You out loud, at first, but know that I am praising You in my heart. In Jesus Name I Pray, With Love and Thanksgiving.

SONGS

Holy, Holy, Holy by Hillsong United
Here For You by Passion
10,000 Reasons by Matt Redman

Hope Found in the Power
of God's Word

Do you ever think that this world is in trouble? Things seem to be going south, and quickly! There is war, evil, self- destruction, self-centered folks who seem to "know it all" (and people actually follow them). Not to mention that "anything goes" these days. . . Well, here is God Breathed Scripture that we all need to live by. It's the advice for daily living.

PROVERBS 2:1-15

My son, if you accept my words and store up my commands within you, turning your ear to wisdom and applying your heart to understanding, and if you call out for insight and cry aloud for understanding, and if you look for it as for silver and search for it as for hidden treasure, then you will understand the fear of the LORD and find the knowledge of God. For the LORD gives wisdom and from his mouth come knowledge and understanding. He holds victory in store for the upright. He is a shield to those whose walk is blameless, for he guards the course of the just and protects the way of his faithful ones. Then you will understand what is right and just and fair—every good path; for wisdom will enter your heart, and knowledge will be pleasant to your soul. Discretion will protect you and understanding will guard you. Wisdom will save you from the ways of wicked men, from men whose words are perverse, who leave the straight paths to walk in dark ways, who delight in doing wrong and rejoice in the perverseness of evil, whose paths are crooked and who are devious in their ways.

PROVERBS 8:17

I love those who love me, and those who seek me find me.

PROVERBS 8:35

For whoever finds me finds life and
receives favor from the LORD.

Basically, God is telling us here, that we are to follow His Word. It's our road map for life; the manual we need to live by. The Tree Of Life! God has made available all that we need, through knowledge in him, including everything in life and godliness (a genuine reverence toward God that governs one's attitude towards every aspect of life). We are called to "Fear the Lord" (reverence for God and reliance on Him). His Word is Godly wisdom and is a virtual "tree of life" that yields the happy life that God fashioned creation to produce. The book of Proverbs mentions "fools or folly". These are folks that say in their heart, "There is no God," therefore they feel free to cruelly prey on others who are at their mercy. I challenge you to read a chapter of Proverbs daily. You have to know what the Bible says if you want to know truth! We also need to feed our faith. It's like a workout or a diet. The more you work out or the more you eat healthy (God given non-processed food), the faster you see results. If you partner a workout and diet together, that's when you receive even more benefits, while speeding up results. The same happens with reading the Bible. You will benefit more if you partner Bible study and Christian radio, along with self –help Christian books and going to church, with reading the Bible daily. BTW ~ Bible Study is electric. There is such energy among believers being together!

We have a choice - we can get into the Word and learn how to live an abundant life, or we can choose to follow this world and live a meaningless life. . As for me ~ I have done both. I followed this world for a long time, friend, and now that I follow Him and learn His ways and pray to walk in His ways ~ ~ There is no comparison and no way would I turn back and live the way I used to. HIS WAY WORKS! I repeat ~ HIS WAY WORKS! I am living proof! You can change your life today, if you need a change of direction, or if your lifestyle is in need of a "pick-me-up", all you have to do is obtain a Bible. If you can't seem to find one, go to the church nearby and ask for one. This could be the first step into a new life that is full of direction, clarity, adventure, abundance, joy, truth, happiness, peace and, perhaps purpose. Who wouldn't want this! You are priceless! He wants only the best for you! God is waiting for you to make that choice today.

~ PRAYER MAY BE SOMETHING LIKE THIS: Okay God, I thought I was ready before, but now I am asking You to write Your Word upon my heart as I seek You, LORD. Empower me, equip me and encourage me to receive Your

Word, understand Your Word, retain Your Word and be obedient to Your Word. I confess that I need a change and would like You to help me, direct me and give me wisdom. Thank You for caring for us; for giving us Your Word that is alive and well, when all we have to do is read it, ponder it day and night and pray that You reveal Your Word to us. I can NOT wait to see the change in me that You are about to do! I'm excited, Lord! Will You do a work in me through Your Word? In Jesus Name I Pray, With Love and Thanksgiving.

SONGS

Word Of God Speak by MercyMe
Awake My Soul by Chris Tomlin
Build My Life by Amanda Cook/Bethel
Your Word by Hillsong Worship

Angela Dee

Hope Found in Spiritual Wisdom

COLOSSIANS 1:9b-14

God to fill you with the knowledge of his will through all spiritual wisdom and understanding. And we pray this in order that you may live a life worthy of the Lord and may please him in every way: bearing fruit in every good work, growing in the knowledge of God, being strengthened with all power according to his glorious might so that you may have great endurance and patience, and joyfully giving thanks to the Father, who has qualified you to share in the inheritance of the saints in the kingdom of light. For he has rescued us form the dominion of darkness and brought us into the kingdom of the Son he loves, in whom we have redemption, the forgiveness of sins.

Do you ever get stuck on where to go from here? Perhaps it's a job change, or lifestyle change, or to move or to wait, to buy, to sell, to marry or divorce, to have children or not, etc. These are life-changing decisions. I know I have been clueless as to what to do next, how to go about it and when. We are called to live a life worthy of the Lord (and not just what "we" want). Sometimes we can get ourselves into unfavorable situations when we don't ask God what "His" will is for us. We need to discern His still small voice. Ask for direction, clarity and when to move or not, so we live a life worthy of the Lord, one that pleases Him. This is a process to learn while reading His Word and asking Him to reveal His Glory to us. Don't be alarmed! He knows our hearts. He'll guide us as long as we stay connected to Him because He cares and wants the best for us. There will be distractions in our lives, so we must be mindful of them and pray to stay focused. His Word, with prayer will direct our steps. I can't say enough about reading His Word daily or even more than once a day, if needed. We simply can't go wrong with His Word. It's our all! We can't grow in His knowledge or be strengthened with His power or receive endurance and patience without reading these scriptures and finding that these are the things we need to pray about and ask Him to bless us according to His will. This is spiritual wisdom and we need to seek it, embrace it, study it and pray to walk in His will. He is there to guide us through anything we pray about. I find comfort and hope in this scripture knowing that He's got it! How about you?

~ PRAYER MAY BE SOMETHING LIKE THIS: Father in Heaven, teach me Your Word. Teach me how to listen to Your voice. Lead me and guide me through this process as I seek Your will. I want what You want Father, so I ask for clarity, In Jesus Name, With Love and Thanksgiving.

SONGS

Be Thou My Vision by Audrey Assad
Turn Your Eyes Upon Jesus by Nichole Nordeman
I Still Believe by Jeremy Camp

Hope Found in Salvation

JOHN 3:16-18

For God so loved the world that he gave his one and only Son, that whoever believes in him shall not perish but have eternal life. For God did not send his Son into the world to condemn the world, but to save the world through him. Whoever believes in him is not condemned, but whoever does not believe stands condemned already because he has not believed in the name of God's one and only Son.

Let's dive into this a minute. . I, myself, need this reminder. Do you? I have seen this scripture taken for granted so many times because we hear it so much! That is sad! We need to be reminded, to stop and take a knee down while meditating on this supreme act of justice! Jesus came into the world to give us eternal life, but it doesn't stop there: (as if that's not enough)! He came into the world to save us and NOT condemn us! He came into the world to Love us and NOT condemn us! He came into the world to Love us, NOT condemn us! Wow! Really? Yes, really!!! Love has won! ! ! It always does! That's the "good news"! The gospel is called "good news" for a reason, my frail friend. . I am frail, weak, broken and sinful. We all are! We are all the same, at the foot of the cross, no matter what! Our debt is paid in full! Hallelujah! However, our thoughts can keep us in bondage, repeating over and over in our minds that we're not good enough, not strong enough, not smart enough, and the list goes on and on. NOTHING COULD BE FURTHER FROM THE TRUTH, no matter what you and I did, or where we are still trying to dig ourselves out of. He knows, but we have to be real with Him and honest. He doesn't expect us to have it all together! He wants our heart, and then, HE GIVES US WHAT IT TAKES to see us through and perhaps do a work in us, as we call on Him. This is free! Oh ~ are you feeling His Unconditional Love yet? You're accepted! You see the worst in yourself while he sees the best! You are worth it! You are chosen! You are set apart! You are precious! You're the apple of his eye! You are amazing and more! Fall into His arms and be held. Have you invited Jesus into your heart? If not, then you can do that right now.

~ PRAYER MAY BE SOMETHING LIKE THIS: Oh Father in heaven, Thank You for sending Your Son into the world to love us and not condemn us. Thank you for being forgiving. I fall short, daily and I need this reminder! Thank You Jesus, for going to the cross for my sins. Thank You for Your mercy and grace. Thank You that Your mercies are new every day. Thank You for making me right with God. I invite You into my heart to be my LORD and Savior. Will You come into my heart and live? In Your Precious Name Jesus, I Pray With Love and Thanksgiving.

SONGS

Resurrection Power by Chris Tomlin
One Who Saves by Hillsong Worship
Hope Of The World by Hillsong Worship
The Stand by Hillsong United
Thank You God For Saving Me by Chris
Tomlin
Redeemed by Big Daddy Weave
Jesus Messiah by Chris Tomlin
We Fall Down by Nicole Nordeman

Hope Found in Purpose

JEREMIAH 29:11-14

"For I know the plans I have for you," declares the LORD, "plans to prosper you and not to harm you, plans to give you hope and a future. Then you will call upon me and come and pray to me, and I will listen to you. You will seek me and find me when you seek me with all your heart. I will be found by you," declares the LORD, "and will bring you back from captivity."

It's time to dream. Dream BIG, friend! God put desires in our hearts, and He wants to use these desires for His plan OR purpose, no matter how big or small our dream is. Bring it to the Lord. He is waiting on us to seek Him with all our heart. He will be found! Go for it! Now! Now our plan will not look like our neighbor's plan, so look to Him and not anyone else. He has a design OR purpose just for "you" and just for me. He's waiting for us to ask Him to join us as we step into action, because He wants to guide us on the journey. There is a bonus to this! It keeps our minds set on Him and not on us and our problems. That my friend is a huge relief!

Here is a tip ~ write down 3 things that you are good at and 1 thing that you are passionate about. Writing things on paper can sometimes help us see our purpose and what comes naturally to us. God can use us in any small way. It doesn't have to be big. It can be as simple as cooking, playing sports, cleaning, organizing, reading, etc. You get the picture! He can use ANYTHING!

~ PRAYER MAY BE SOMETHING LIKE THIS: My God, Thank You for this dream/plan in me. Show me the steps to take, large or small and one day at a time, to achieve this desire. This can be such an exciting time in my life! Equip me and encourage me to walk in Your Will through this journey. I ask that you use me for Your glory, Lord. In Your Name I Pray, Jesus, With Love and Thanksgiving.

SONGS

Dream Small by Josh Wilson
I Will Follow by Chris Tomlin
God Help Me by Plumb

Hope Found in Serving Our Lord

Do you find yourself trying to make everyone "happy" around you? Are you a "people pleaser"? I know that I have fallen into this trap (more than once). I just want everyone to get along! Sometimes I just want some peace! The good news is ~ we can have peace!

GALATIANS 1:10b

If I were still trying to please men, I
would not be a servant of Christ

I don't know about you, but I love this scripture! It is freeing that I can be "myself" around folks! I don't have to try to measure up or keep everyone together or please them the way they may want me to please them or even serve them! I'm not talking about being disobedient here. I am implying that some folks want you and me to be a certain way to please "them"! That's not our job! God is calling us to serve "Him" (not others). We are called to love them.

We are called to serve God. Not to go through life aimlessly. . We all have a gift in us that we are called to share with the world (to make the world a better place), no matter how ineffective we think we are. We are called to live with "purpose". . .Maybe that could be serving in a soup kitchen, or babysitting for someone in need, helping out in a small or large way, someone who is lonely or doesn't have anyone else to count on. . .The list is endless! I do want to point out that when He calls us to serve, it will be in His timing and not ours. In other words, it's not always going to be a convenient time for us, yet we need to be willing to step up to the plate when He calls us. This is another way that one can see how we believers are set apart from this world (by being the hands n feet of Jesus).

~ PRAYER MAY BE SOMETHING LIKE THIS: Gracious Heavenly Father will you show me the gift(s) that you put in me? I'm not really sure what they are. How can I make a difference? You set me free from my sin by the redemption that is in Christ and I want to serve You and give back to You for setting me free. I don't deserve this gift. Will you show me how I can make a difference in this world that You love? I pray this in Jesus Name, With Love and Thanksgiving.

~ Maybe you can get a team of folks together to come along side of you to serve. Make it a fun experience with a good heart and loving attitude. The world will be a better place because you do your part and serve the Lord. I believe that He is sure to love your big heart and you will make a difference!

SONGS

God Of This City by Chris Tomlin
These Hands by Jeff Deyo
Shine by Matt Redman

Hope Found in Heaven

2 TIMOTHY 4:18

The Lord will rescue me from every evil attack
and will bring me safely to his heavenly kingdom.
To him be glory for ever and ever. Amen.

Finally, what a relief! We have a new home to look forward to! Life doesn't end here. We have eternity to look forward to! No weeping will be heard! Pure joy awaits us! We will be with our King forever!

My picture of me in heaven is, me wrapped in his loving arms with the biggest, tightest hug imaginable! I believe I will be thanking Jesus and praising Jesus with unending tears of joy, while enjoying his presence, enthralled in all the beauty that heaven has to offer, as well as seeing my loved ones again. What a reunion!!!

What about you? Have you taken time to meditate on your future? I sure hope so! There is unending forthcoming for you, when you step into glory. I pray that you take Jesus' hand as he reaches out for your hand on the day he calls you home. Oh what joy! What a reunion!

SONGS

This One's With Me by NewSong
Soon And Very Soon by Hillsong Worship
I Will Rise by Chris Tomlin
I Can Only Imagine by MercyMe
Endless Hallelujah by Matt Redman

EPHESIANS 6:10

Finally, be strong in the Lord and in his mighty power.

ROMANS 15:13

May the God of hope fill you with all joy and
peace as you trust in him, so that you may overflow
with hope by the power of the Holy Spirit.

PHILIPPIANS 2:1-5

If you have any encouragement from being united with
Christ, if any comfort from his love, if any fellowship with
the Spirit, if any tenderness and compassion, then make my
joy complete by being like- minded, having love, being one
in spirit and purpose. Do nothing out of selfish ambition
or vain conceit, but in humility consider others better than
yourselves. Each of you should look not only to your own
interests, but also to the interests of others. Your attitude
should be the same as that of Christ Jesus.

Summary

1. GET INTO THE WORD. MAKE IT A DAILY PART OF YOUR LIFE (morning if possible).
2. GET PLUGGED INTO A CHURCH THAT IS A GOOD FIT FOR YOU.
3. GET CONNECTED WITH OTHER BELIEVERS, IN COMMUNITY GROUPS/ BIBLE STUDY.
4. SURROUND YOURSELF WITH CHRISTIAN RADIO, TV, MUSIC, BOOKS, ETC. (it's out there).
5. VOLUNTEER AND SERVE THE LORD. THERE IS DEEP NEED AND THAT HELPS KEEP YOU FOCUSED.

LET'S PRAY FOR ONE ANOTHER DAILY. FOR WE'RE ALL IN THIS BATTLE TOGETHER

God penned these scriptures, songs and thoughts on my heart, to be an encouragement for you. It is my deepest prayer that you are open to what He has in store for you; That you delve into His Word during unrushed time; That he breathes life in you through His Word; That you find the love of your life in Him; that you discover your God given purpose; that you believe your worth; that you leave a legacy and that you love Him with an undying love.

happy journey !

Resources

AVAILABLE BELOW, ARE RECOMMENDATIONS
FOUND ON RADIO, T V, ON-LINE
OR AT YOUR LOCAL LIBRARY.

KLOVE contemporary Christian music is on F M radio in many cities across the U S. There are local radio stations on both A M and F M radio that have encouraging messages as well as music.

Focus on the Family; Helping families thrive
www.focusonthefamily.com 1-800-A-FAMILY

New Life Christian Counselors www.newlife.com 1-800 New-Life

Bible Studies are available at Christian book stores and on-line

Christian Books are available at Christian book stores, library and on-line

Pastors and Speakers are available on-line, radio and television that can help you to stay connected while growing in your faith.

COUNT YOUR BLESSINGS / JOURNAL

I encourage you to write down your blessings, prayers answered and daily strengths found in the Lord. These will be your reminders of how God has been working in your life. It's a thrill to look back and view all of the ways that God has been showing you His Glory!

Printed in the United States
By Bookmasters